50 Satisfying Vegan Burgers and Sandwiches

By: Kelly Johnson

Table of Contents

- Classic Black Bean Burger
- Chickpea and Avocado Sandwich
- Sweet Potato and Black Bean Burger
- Portobello Mushroom Burger
- BBQ Tempeh Sandwich
- Lentil and Mushroom Burger
- Falafel Pita Sandwich
- Spicy Chickpea Burger
- Vegan Sloppy Joes
- BBQ Jackfruit Sandwich
- Cauliflower Buffalo Wings Sandwich
- Tofu Banh Mi
- Vegan BLT with Tempeh Bacon
- Peanut Butter and Banana Veggie Burger
- Quinoa and Beet Burger
- Sweet Potato and Chickpea Burger
- Grilled Veggie and Hummus Sandwich
- Avocado and Chickpea Salad Sandwich
- Zucchini Fritter Burger
- Vegan "Chicken" Caesar Sandwich
- Curried Chickpea Sandwich
- Vegan Reuben Sandwich
- Tempeh and Avocado Sandwich
- Veggie Burger with Cashew Cheese
- Tofu and Avocado Wrap
- Spicy Lentil and Walnut Burger
- Mushroom and Walnut Burger
- Thai Peanut Tempeh Sandwich
- Vegan Philly Cheesesteak
- Tempeh BBQ Burger
- Grilled Eggplant and Pesto Sandwich
- Vegan Tofu Club Sandwich
- Chickpea and Cucumber Sandwich
- Seitan Cheeseburger
- BBQ Veggie Burger

- Vegan Avocado and Tofu Wrap
- Tempeh Lettuce and Tomato Sandwich
- Veggie "Tuna" Salad Sandwich
- Portobello and Spinach Burger
- Chickpea and Spinach Burger
- Vegan Meatball Sub
- Roasted Carrot and Hummus Sandwich
- Crispy Tofu and Coleslaw Sandwich
- Black Bean and Quinoa Burger
- Vegan Buffalo Cauliflower Sandwich
- Grilled Tofu and Veggie Wrap
- Smoky Chickpea Burger
- Cauliflower and Chickpea Sandwich
- Seitan and Avocado Burger
- Vegan Lentil Burger

Classic Black Bean Burger

Ingredients:

- 1 can (15 oz) black beans, drained and rinsed
- 1/2 cup breadcrumbs (or gluten-free breadcrumbs)
- 1/4 cup finely chopped onion
- 1/4 cup grated carrot
- 1/4 cup chopped cilantro
- 1 tbsp soy sauce or tamari
- 1 tsp garlic powder
- 1 tsp cumin
- Salt and pepper to taste
- Olive oil for cooking

Instructions:

1. **Mash**: In a bowl, mash the black beans with a fork or potato masher, leaving some chunks for texture.
2. **Mix**: Add breadcrumbs, onion, carrot, cilantro, soy sauce, garlic powder, cumin, salt, and pepper. Stir until well combined.
3. **Shape**: Form the mixture into 4 patties.
4. **Cook**: Heat olive oil in a skillet over medium heat. Cook the patties for about 4-5 minutes per side, until golden brown.
5. **Serve**: Serve on buns with your favorite toppings like lettuce, tomato, and avocado.

Chickpea and Avocado Sandwich

Ingredients:

- 1 can (15 oz) chickpeas, drained and rinsed
- 1 ripe avocado
- 1 tbsp lemon juice
- 1/4 cup tahini
- 1/4 tsp garlic powder
- Salt and pepper to taste
- 2 slices whole grain bread
- Lettuce, tomato, and cucumber slices for garnish

Instructions:

1. **Mash**: In a bowl, mash the chickpeas and avocado together until creamy.
2. **Mix**: Stir in lemon juice, tahini, garlic powder, salt, and pepper.
3. **Assemble**: Spread the mixture on one slice of bread and top with lettuce, tomato, and cucumber.
4. **Serve**: Top with the second slice of bread and serve.

Sweet Potato and Black Bean Burger

Ingredients:

- 1 medium sweet potato, peeled and cubed
- 1 can (15 oz) black beans, drained and rinsed
- 1/2 cup breadcrumbs (or gluten-free breadcrumbs)
- 1/4 cup finely chopped onion
- 1 tsp cumin
- 1/2 tsp smoked paprika
- 1 tbsp olive oil
- Salt and pepper to taste

Instructions:

1. **Cook Sweet Potato**: Boil or steam the sweet potato cubes until soft, about 10-12 minutes. Mash them in a bowl.
2. **Mix**: Add black beans, breadcrumbs, onion, cumin, smoked paprika, olive oil, salt, and pepper. Stir until everything is combined.
3. **Shape**: Form the mixture into 4 patties.
4. **Cook**: Heat olive oil in a skillet over medium heat. Cook the patties for about 4-5 minutes per side, until golden brown.
5. **Serve**: Serve on buns with your favorite toppings.

Portobello Mushroom Burger

Ingredients:

- 4 large portobello mushroom caps, stems removed
- 2 tbsp balsamic vinegar
- 1 tbsp olive oil
- 1 tsp garlic powder
- Salt and pepper to taste
- 4 burger buns
- Lettuce, tomato, and cheese for topping

Instructions:

1. **Marinate**: In a bowl, mix balsamic vinegar, olive oil, garlic powder, salt, and pepper. Brush the mushroom caps with the marinade and let them sit for 10 minutes.
2. **Grill**: Grill the mushrooms on medium heat for 5-7 minutes per side, until tender.
3. **Assemble**: Place the grilled mushrooms on buns and top with lettuce, tomato, and cheese.
4. **Serve**: Serve immediately.

BBQ Tempeh Sandwich

Ingredients:

- 1 block tempeh, sliced thinly
- 1/4 cup BBQ sauce
- 1 tbsp olive oil
- 2 sandwich buns
- Coleslaw for garnish (optional)

Instructions:

1. **Cook Tempeh**: Heat olive oil in a skillet over medium heat. Cook the tempeh slices for 4-5 minutes on each side until golden brown.
2. **Add Sauce**: Pour the BBQ sauce over the tempeh and cook for another 2-3 minutes, allowing the sauce to heat through.
3. **Assemble**: Place the BBQ tempeh on buns and top with coleslaw if desired.
4. **Serve**: Serve immediately.

Lentil and Mushroom Burger

Ingredients:

- 1 cup cooked lentils
- 1/2 cup finely chopped mushrooms
- 1/4 cup breadcrumbs (or gluten-free breadcrumbs)
- 1 tbsp soy sauce or tamari
- 1/4 tsp garlic powder
- 1/4 tsp thyme
- Olive oil for cooking

Instructions:

1. **Cook Mushrooms**: Sauté the mushrooms in olive oil over medium heat until softened, about 5 minutes.
2. **Mix**: In a bowl, combine cooked lentils, sautéed mushrooms, breadcrumbs, soy sauce, garlic powder, and thyme. Mash the mixture together.
3. **Shape**: Form the mixture into 4 patties.
4. **Cook**: Heat olive oil in a skillet over medium heat. Cook the patties for about 4-5 minutes per side, until golden brown.
5. **Serve**: Serve on buns with your favorite toppings.

Falafel Pita Sandwich

Ingredients:

- 1 can (15 oz) chickpeas, drained and rinsed
- 1/4 cup finely chopped onion
- 1/4 cup fresh parsley
- 1 tbsp tahini
- 1 tsp cumin
- 1 tsp coriander
- 2 cloves garlic, minced
- Salt and pepper to taste
- 1 tbsp olive oil
- 4 pita breads
- Toppings: cucumber, tomato, lettuce, tahini sauce

Instructions:

1. **Blend**: In a food processor, combine chickpeas, onion, parsley, tahini, cumin, coriander, garlic, salt, and pepper. Blend until smooth.
2. **Form Balls**: Form the mixture into small balls or patties.
3. **Cook**: Heat olive oil in a skillet over medium heat. Fry the falafel for 3-4 minutes per side, until golden brown.
4. **Assemble**: Place the falafel in pita pockets and top with cucumber, tomato, lettuce, and tahini sauce.
5. **Serve**: Serve immediately.

Spicy Chickpea Burger

Ingredients:

- 1 can (15 oz) chickpeas, drained and rinsed
- 1/4 cup breadcrumbs (or gluten-free breadcrumbs)
- 1/4 cup finely chopped onion
- 1 tbsp sriracha or hot sauce
- 1 tsp cumin
- 1/4 tsp smoked paprika
- Salt and pepper to taste
- Olive oil for cooking

Instructions:

1. **Mash**: In a bowl, mash the chickpeas with a fork or potato masher, leaving some chunks for texture.
2. **Mix**: Add breadcrumbs, onion, sriracha, cumin, smoked paprika, salt, and pepper. Stir to combine.
3. **Shape**: Form the mixture into 4 patties.
4. **Cook**: Heat olive oil in a skillet over medium heat. Cook the patties for about 4-5 minutes per side, until golden brown.
5. **Serve**: Serve on buns with lettuce, tomato, and your favorite condiments.

Vegan Sloppy Joes

Ingredients:

- 1 can (15 oz) lentils or kidney beans, drained and rinsed
- 1 tbsp olive oil
- 1 small onion, finely chopped
- 1 bell pepper, finely chopped
- 2 cloves garlic, minced
- 1 cup tomato sauce
- 1 tbsp soy sauce or tamari
- 2 tbsp maple syrup
- 1 tbsp apple cider vinegar
- 1 tsp smoked paprika
- 1/2 tsp chili powder
- Salt and pepper to taste
- 4 sandwich buns

Instructions:

1. **Sauté Vegetables**: Heat olive oil in a skillet over medium heat. Add the onion, bell pepper, and garlic. Sauté for 5-7 minutes until softened.
2. **Add Beans**: Stir in the lentils or beans, tomato sauce, soy sauce, maple syrup, apple cider vinegar, smoked paprika, chili powder, salt, and pepper. Simmer for 10-15 minutes, until the sauce thickens.
3. **Assemble**: Spoon the sloppy joe mixture onto buns and serve hot.

BBQ Jackfruit Sandwich

Ingredients:

- 2 cans (15 oz) young green jackfruit in brine, drained and shredded
- 1 tbsp olive oil
- 1 small onion, finely chopped
- 2 cloves garlic, minced
- 1 cup BBQ sauce
- 1/2 cup vegetable broth
- 1 tsp smoked paprika
- Salt and pepper to taste
- 4 sandwich buns
- Coleslaw for garnish (optional)

Instructions:

1. **Prepare Jackfruit**: Drain and shred the jackfruit with your hands or a fork to resemble pulled pork.
2. **Sauté Vegetables**: Heat olive oil in a skillet over medium heat. Add onion and garlic, and sauté until softened.
3. **Cook Jackfruit**: Add the shredded jackfruit, BBQ sauce, vegetable broth, smoked paprika, salt, and pepper. Simmer for 15-20 minutes, until the mixture thickens and the jackfruit absorbs the flavors.
4. **Assemble**: Spoon the BBQ jackfruit onto buns and top with coleslaw if desired.

Cauliflower Buffalo Wings Sandwich

Ingredients:

- 1 small head of cauliflower, cut into florets
- 1 cup flour (or chickpea flour for a gluten-free option)
- 1/2 cup water
- 1 tsp garlic powder
- 1 tsp smoked paprika
- Salt and pepper to taste
- 1 cup buffalo sauce
- 4 sandwich buns
- Lettuce and tomato for garnish

Instructions:

1. **Prepare Cauliflower**: Preheat oven to 400°F (200°C). In a bowl, whisk together flour, water, garlic powder, smoked paprika, salt, and pepper. Dip cauliflower florets in the batter, then place on a baking sheet lined with parchment paper.
2. **Bake**: Bake cauliflower for 20 minutes, flipping halfway through, until crispy.
3. **Coat in Buffalo Sauce**: Toss the baked cauliflower in buffalo sauce.
4. **Assemble**: Place the buffalo cauliflower on buns and top with lettuce, tomato, and any other desired toppings.

Tofu Banh Mi

Ingredients:

- 1 block firm tofu, pressed and sliced
- 1 tbsp soy sauce or tamari
- 1 tbsp rice vinegar
- 1 tbsp maple syrup
- 1/2 tsp garlic powder
- 1/2 cucumber, thinly sliced
- 1 small carrot, julienned
- Fresh cilantro
- 1-2 baguettes or sandwich rolls
- Vegan mayo for spread (optional)

Instructions:

1. **Marinate Tofu**: In a small bowl, mix soy sauce, rice vinegar, maple syrup, and garlic powder. Marinate tofu slices in the mixture for at least 15 minutes.
2. **Cook Tofu**: Heat a skillet over medium heat and cook the tofu for 3-4 minutes on each side, until golden brown.
3. **Assemble**: Spread vegan mayo (if using) on the baguette. Layer tofu, cucumber, carrot, and cilantro on the bread.
4. **Serve**: Serve immediately, garnished with extra cilantro.

Vegan BLT with Tempeh Bacon

Ingredients:

- 1 block tempeh, sliced thinly
- 2 tbsp soy sauce or tamari
- 1 tbsp maple syrup
- 1 tsp smoked paprika
- 1 tsp liquid smoke (optional)
- 4 slices whole grain bread
- Lettuce, tomato, and avocado for garnish
- Vegan mayo (optional)

Instructions:

1. **Prepare Tempeh Bacon**: In a bowl, whisk together soy sauce, maple syrup, smoked paprika, and liquid smoke. Marinate the tempeh slices in the mixture for at least 15 minutes.
2. **Cook Tempeh**: Heat a skillet over medium heat and cook the tempeh for 3-4 minutes on each side, until crispy.
3. **Assemble**: Spread vegan mayo (if using) on the bread. Layer the tempeh bacon, lettuce, tomato, and avocado on the bread.
4. **Serve**: Serve immediately.

Peanut Butter and Banana Veggie Burger

Ingredients:

- 1 can (15 oz) chickpeas, drained and rinsed
- 1/4 cup peanut butter
- 1 ripe banana, mashed
- 1/4 cup breadcrumbs (or gluten-free breadcrumbs)
- 1 tbsp maple syrup
- 1/2 tsp cinnamon
- 1/4 tsp nutmeg
- Salt and pepper to taste
- Olive oil for cooking
- 4 sandwich buns

Instructions:

1. **Mix**: In a bowl, mash the chickpeas, peanut butter, banana, maple syrup, cinnamon, nutmeg, salt, and pepper. Stir in breadcrumbs until well combined.
2. **Shape**: Form the mixture into 4 patties.
3. **Cook**: Heat olive oil in a skillet over medium heat. Cook the patties for 4-5 minutes on each side, until golden brown.
4. **Serve**: Serve on buns with your favorite toppings.

Quinoa and Beet Burger

Ingredients:

- 1 cup cooked quinoa
- 1 small beetroot, grated
- 1/4 cup breadcrumbs (or gluten-free breadcrumbs)
- 1/4 cup finely chopped onion
- 1 tbsp soy sauce or tamari
- 1 tsp ground cumin
- Salt and pepper to taste
- Olive oil for cooking
- 4 sandwich buns

Instructions:

1. **Mix**: In a bowl, combine quinoa, grated beetroot, breadcrumbs, onion, soy sauce, cumin, salt, and pepper. Stir until everything is well mixed.
2. **Shape**: Form the mixture into 4 patties.
3. **Cook**: Heat olive oil in a skillet over medium heat. Cook the patties for 4-5 minutes on each side, until golden brown.
4. **Serve**: Serve on buns with your favorite toppings.

Sweet Potato and Chickpea Burger

Ingredients:

- 1 medium sweet potato, peeled and cubed
- 1 can (15 oz) chickpeas, drained and rinsed
- 1/4 cup breadcrumbs (or gluten-free breadcrumbs)
- 1/4 cup finely chopped onion
- 1 tsp cumin
- 1/2 tsp smoked paprika
- Salt and pepper to taste
- Olive oil for cooking
- 4 sandwich buns

Instructions:

1. **Cook Sweet Potato**: Boil or steam the sweet potato cubes until soft, about 10-12 minutes. Mash them in a bowl.
2. **Mix**: Add chickpeas, breadcrumbs, onion, cumin, smoked paprika, salt, and pepper. Mash together until combined but still a bit chunky.
3. **Shape**: Form the mixture into 4 patties.
4. **Cook**: Heat olive oil in a skillet over medium heat. Cook the patties for 4-5 minutes per side, until golden brown.
5. **Serve**: Serve on buns with your favorite toppings.

Grilled Veggie and Hummus Sandwich

Ingredients:

- 2 slices whole grain bread
- 1/4 cup hummus
- 1/4 cup roasted red bell peppers, sliced
- 1/4 cup grilled zucchini, sliced
- 1/4 cup grilled eggplant, sliced
- Fresh spinach or arugula
- Olive oil for grilling

Instructions:

1. **Prepare Veggies**: Grill the zucchini, eggplant, and red bell peppers on a grill pan or outdoor grill until softened and lightly charred.
2. **Assemble Sandwich**: Spread hummus on one slice of bread. Layer the grilled vegetables and fresh spinach or arugula on top.
3. **Grill**: Drizzle olive oil on the outside of the sandwich and grill in a panini press or on a skillet over medium heat for 3-5 minutes per side, until golden and crispy.
4. **Serve**: Serve warm.

Avocado and Chickpea Salad Sandwich

Ingredients:

- 1 can (15 oz) chickpeas, drained and mashed
- 1 ripe avocado, mashed
- 1 tbsp lemon juice
- 1 tbsp olive oil
- 1/2 tsp garlic powder
- Salt and pepper to taste
- Fresh cilantro or parsley, chopped
- 2 slices whole grain bread

Instructions:

1. **Prepare Salad**: In a bowl, mash the chickpeas and avocado together. Add lemon juice, olive oil, garlic powder, salt, and pepper. Stir in the chopped cilantro or parsley.
2. **Assemble Sandwich**: Spread the chickpea and avocado mixture onto one slice of bread. Top with the second slice of bread.
3. **Serve**: Serve immediately or refrigerate for later.

Zucchini Fritter Burger

Ingredients:

- 2 medium zucchinis, grated
- 1/2 cup breadcrumbs
- 1/4 cup grated vegan cheese (optional)
- 1/4 cup flour (or chickpea flour)
- 1/2 tsp garlic powder
- Salt and pepper to taste
- Olive oil for cooking
- 4 sandwich buns
- Fresh lettuce and tomato for garnish

Instructions:

1. **Prepare Fritter Mixture**: Grate the zucchinis and squeeze out excess moisture using a clean kitchen towel. In a bowl, combine grated zucchini, breadcrumbs, flour, garlic powder, salt, and pepper.
2. **Form Patties**: Shape the mixture into 4 patties.
3. **Cook**: Heat olive oil in a skillet over medium heat. Cook the fritters for 3-4 minutes on each side, until golden and crispy.
4. **Assemble Sandwich**: Place the fritters on the sandwich buns and garnish with fresh lettuce, tomato, and any other desired toppings.
5. **Serve**: Serve hot.

Vegan "Chicken" Caesar Sandwich

Ingredients:

- 1 block firm tofu, pressed and sliced into strips
- 1/4 cup olive oil
- 2 tbsp soy sauce or tamari
- 1 tbsp nutritional yeast
- 1 tsp garlic powder
- 1/2 tsp smoked paprika
- 2 cups romaine lettuce, chopped
- 2 tbsp vegan Caesar dressing
- 4 sandwich buns

Instructions:

1. **Prepare Vegan Chicken**: In a bowl, mix olive oil, soy sauce, nutritional yeast, garlic powder, and smoked paprika. Toss the tofu strips in the marinade and let sit for 10-15 minutes.
2. **Cook Tofu**: Heat a skillet over medium heat and cook the marinated tofu strips for 4-5 minutes on each side, until crispy and golden.
3. **Assemble Sandwich**: Toss the chopped lettuce with vegan Caesar dressing. Place the tofu "chicken" and dressed lettuce on the sandwich buns.
4. **Serve**: Serve immediately.

Curried Chickpea Sandwich

Ingredients:

- 1 can (15 oz) chickpeas, drained and mashed
- 2 tbsp vegan mayo
- 1 tbsp curry powder
- 1 tbsp lemon juice
- 1/2 tsp garlic powder
- Salt and pepper to taste
- Fresh cilantro, chopped
- 2 slices whole grain bread

Instructions:

1. **Prepare Chickpea Salad**: In a bowl, mash the chickpeas and mix with vegan mayo, curry powder, lemon juice, garlic powder, salt, and pepper.
2. **Assemble Sandwich**: Spread the curried chickpea mixture onto one slice of bread. Top with the second slice of bread.
3. **Serve**: Serve immediately or refrigerate for later.

Vegan Reuben Sandwich

Ingredients:

- 1 block tempeh, sliced into thin strips
- 1 tbsp soy sauce or tamari
- 1 tbsp maple syrup
- 1 tsp smoked paprika
- 2 slices rye bread
- 1/4 cup vegan thousand island dressing
- 1/4 cup sauerkraut
- Fresh spinach or lettuce

Instructions:

1. **Prepare Tempeh**: In a bowl, mix soy sauce, maple syrup, and smoked paprika. Marinate the tempeh slices for 10-15 minutes.
2. **Cook Tempeh**: Heat a skillet over medium heat and cook the tempeh for 3-4 minutes on each side, until golden brown.
3. **Assemble Sandwich**: Spread vegan thousand island dressing on one slice of rye bread. Layer tempeh, sauerkraut, and spinach or lettuce. Top with the second slice of rye bread.
4. **Grill**: Grill the sandwich in a skillet or panini press until crispy and golden on both sides.
5. **Serve**: Serve hot.

Tempeh and Avocado Sandwich

Ingredients:

- 1 block tempeh, sliced thinly
- 1 avocado, mashed
- 1 tbsp soy sauce or tamari
- 1 tbsp olive oil
- 1/2 tsp garlic powder
- Salt and pepper to taste
- 2 slices whole grain bread
- Fresh spinach or lettuce

Instructions:

1. **Prepare Tempeh**: In a bowl, mix soy sauce, olive oil, garlic powder, salt, and pepper. Marinate the tempeh slices for 10-15 minutes.
2. **Cook Tempeh**: Heat a skillet over medium heat and cook the tempeh for 3-4 minutes on each side, until crispy.
3. **Assemble Sandwich**: Spread mashed avocado on one slice of bread. Layer the cooked tempeh and fresh spinach or lettuce on top. Top with the second slice of bread.
4. **Serve**: Serve immediately.

Veggie Burger with Cashew Cheese

Ingredients:

- 1 can (15 oz) black beans, drained and mashed
- 1/2 cup grated carrots
- 1/4 cup breadcrumbs
- 1 tbsp soy sauce or tamari
- 1/2 tsp cumin
- 1/2 tsp smoked paprika
- Salt and pepper to taste
- 1/2 cup cashews, soaked and blended into a creamy cheese sauce
- 4 sandwich buns

Instructions:

1. **Prepare Veggie Patty**: In a bowl, mix mashed black beans, grated carrots, breadcrumbs, soy sauce, cumin, smoked paprika, salt, and pepper. Shape the mixture into 4 patties.
2. **Cook Patties**: Heat a skillet over medium heat and cook the patties for 3-4 minutes on each side, until golden brown.
3. **Prepare Cashew Cheese**: In a blender, combine soaked cashews with a bit of water, salt, and nutritional yeast to make a creamy cheese sauce.
4. **Assemble Sandwich**: Place the veggie patty on the sandwich bun and top with cashew cheese.
5. **Serve**: Serve hot with your favorite toppings.

Tofu and Avocado Wrap

Ingredients:

- 1 block firm tofu, pressed and sliced
- 1 ripe avocado, sliced
- 1 tbsp soy sauce or tamari
- 1 tbsp olive oil
- 1 tsp garlic powder
- 1/2 tsp smoked paprika
- 1 large whole wheat tortilla
- Fresh spinach or lettuce
- 1/4 cup hummus

Instructions:

1. **Prepare Tofu**: Marinate the tofu slices in soy sauce, olive oil, garlic powder, and smoked paprika for 10 minutes.
2. **Cook Tofu**: Heat a skillet over medium heat and cook the tofu slices for 3-4 minutes on each side, until golden and crispy.
3. **Assemble Wrap**: Lay the tortilla flat and spread hummus on it. Add tofu slices, avocado, and fresh spinach or lettuce.
4. **Wrap and Serve**: Roll up the tortilla to enclose the fillings and serve immediately.

Spicy Lentil and Walnut Burger

Ingredients:

- 1 cup cooked lentils
- 1/2 cup walnuts, finely chopped
- 1/2 cup breadcrumbs
- 1/4 cup grated carrot
- 1 tbsp soy sauce or tamari
- 1 tbsp sriracha sauce
- 1/2 tsp cumin
- Salt and pepper to taste
- 4 sandwich buns
- Lettuce, tomato, and vegan mayo for garnish

Instructions:

1. **Prepare Burger Mixture**: In a food processor, combine cooked lentils, chopped walnuts, breadcrumbs, grated carrot, soy sauce, sriracha sauce, cumin, salt, and pepper. Pulse until the mixture comes together.
2. **Form Patties**: Shape the mixture into 4 patties.
3. **Cook Patties**: Heat a skillet over medium heat and cook the patties for 4-5 minutes on each side, until golden brown.
4. **Assemble Burger**: Place the patty on the sandwich bun and add lettuce, tomato, and vegan mayo.
5. **Serve**: Serve hot.

Mushroom and Walnut Burger

Ingredients:

- 1 cup mushrooms, finely chopped
- 1/2 cup walnuts, finely chopped
- 1/2 cup breadcrumbs
- 1 tbsp soy sauce or tamari
- 1/2 tsp thyme
- 1/4 cup grated vegan cheese (optional)
- Salt and pepper to taste
- 4 sandwich buns
- Fresh lettuce, tomato, and vegan mayo for garnish

Instructions:

1. **Prepare Burger Mixture**: In a pan, sauté the mushrooms until they release their moisture and become soft. Let them cool. In a bowl, combine the mushrooms, walnuts, breadcrumbs, soy sauce, thyme, vegan cheese (optional), salt, and pepper. Mix until the mixture holds together.
2. **Form Patties**: Shape the mixture into 4 patties.
3. **Cook Patties**: Heat a skillet over medium heat and cook the patties for 4-5 minutes on each side, until crispy and golden brown.
4. **Assemble Burger**: Place the patty on the sandwich bun and add fresh lettuce, tomato, and vegan mayo.
5. **Serve**: Serve hot.

Thai Peanut Tempeh Sandwich

Ingredients:

- 1 block tempeh, sliced
- 1/4 cup peanut butter
- 2 tbsp soy sauce or tamari
- 1 tbsp maple syrup
- 1 tsp lime juice
- 1/2 tsp ginger powder
- 1/4 cup shredded carrots
- Fresh cilantro
- 4 sandwich buns

Instructions:

1. **Prepare Tempeh**: Slice the tempeh and marinate in a mixture of peanut butter, soy sauce, maple syrup, lime juice, and ginger powder for 15-20 minutes.
2. **Cook Tempeh**: Heat a skillet over medium heat and cook the marinated tempeh for 4-5 minutes on each side, until golden.
3. **Assemble Sandwich**: Place tempeh on the sandwich buns, then top with shredded carrots and fresh cilantro.
4. **Serve**: Serve immediately.

Vegan Philly Cheesesteak

Ingredients:

- 1 block seitan, sliced thinly (or mushrooms for a lighter version)
- 1 onion, sliced
- 1 bell pepper, sliced
- 1 tbsp soy sauce or tamari
- 1 tbsp olive oil
- 1/4 cup vegan cheese (optional)
- 4 sandwich hoagie rolls
- Fresh spinach (optional)

Instructions:

1. **Cook Veggies**: In a skillet, heat olive oil over medium heat. Sauté the onions and bell peppers until soft and caramelized.
2. **Cook Seitan**: Add the seitan (or mushrooms) to the skillet and sauté for 3-4 minutes until heated through. Add soy sauce and cook for another minute.
3. **Assemble Sandwich**: Place the seitan and veggie mixture into hoagie rolls. Add vegan cheese if desired, and top with fresh spinach.
4. **Serve**: Serve hot.

Tempeh BBQ Burger

Ingredients:

- 1 block tempeh, sliced into patties
- 1/2 cup BBQ sauce (vegan)
- 1 tbsp olive oil
- 4 sandwich buns
- Lettuce, tomato, and pickles for garnish

Instructions:

1. **Marinate Tempeh**: Marinate the tempeh patties in BBQ sauce for at least 30 minutes.
2. **Cook Tempeh**: Heat olive oil in a skillet over medium heat and cook the tempeh for 4-5 minutes on each side, until crispy and heated through.
3. **Assemble Burger**: Place tempeh on sandwich buns and add lettuce, tomato, and pickles.
4. **Serve**: Serve immediately.

Grilled Eggplant and Pesto Sandwich

Ingredients:

- 1 eggplant, sliced into rounds
- 2 tbsp olive oil
- Salt and pepper to taste
- 2 tbsp vegan pesto sauce
- 4 sandwich rolls or slices of bread
- Fresh spinach or arugula

Instructions:

1. **Prepare Eggplant**: Preheat the grill or grill pan. Drizzle eggplant slices with olive oil, salt, and pepper. Grill for 3-4 minutes on each side, until softened and charred.
2. **Assemble Sandwich**: Spread pesto sauce on sandwich rolls or bread. Layer with grilled eggplant and fresh spinach or arugula.
3. **Serve**: Serve immediately.

Vegan Tofu Club Sandwich

Ingredients:

- 1 block firm tofu, pressed and sliced
- 2 tbsp soy sauce or tamari
- 1 tbsp olive oil
- 1 tsp smoked paprika
- 1/4 cup vegan mayo
- Lettuce and tomato slices
- 4 slices whole grain bread, toasted

Instructions:

1. **Prepare Tofu**: Marinate tofu slices in soy sauce, olive oil, and smoked paprika for 10 minutes.
2. **Cook Tofu**: Heat a skillet over medium heat and cook the tofu for 3-4 minutes on each side, until golden.
3. **Assemble Sandwich**: Spread vegan mayo on the toasted bread slices. Layer with tofu, lettuce, and tomato.
4. **Serve**: Serve immediately.

Chickpea and Cucumber Sandwich

Ingredients:

- 1 can chickpeas, drained and mashed
- 1/2 cucumber, thinly sliced
- 2 tbsp vegan mayo
- 1 tbsp lemon juice
- Salt and pepper to taste
- 4 slices whole grain bread
- Fresh dill (optional)

Instructions:

1. **Prepare Filling**: Mash the chickpeas in a bowl and mix with vegan mayo, lemon juice, salt, and pepper.
2. **Assemble Sandwich**: Spread the chickpea mixture on two slices of bread. Layer with cucumber slices and garnish with fresh dill, if desired.
3. **Serve**: Top with the remaining bread slice and serve immediately.

Seitan Cheeseburger

Ingredients:

- 1 block seitan, sliced into patties
- 1/4 cup vegan cheese (optional)
- 1 tbsp soy sauce or tamari
- 1 tbsp olive oil
- 4 sandwich buns
- Lettuce, tomato, pickles, and vegan mayo for garnish

Instructions:

1. **Cook Seitan**: Heat olive oil in a skillet over medium heat. Add seitan patties and cook for 4-5 minutes on each side until crispy. Add a slice of vegan cheese during the last minute of cooking to melt.
2. **Assemble Burger**: Place seitan patties on sandwich buns and add lettuce, tomato, pickles, and vegan mayo.
3. **Serve**: Serve immediately.

BBQ Veggie Burger

Ingredients:

- 1 cup cooked black beans, mashed
- 1/2 cup breadcrumbs
- 1/2 cup grated carrot
- 1/4 cup corn kernels
- 2 tbsp BBQ sauce
- 1 tsp smoked paprika
- Salt and pepper to taste
- 4 sandwich buns
- Lettuce, tomato, and avocado for garnish

Instructions:

1. **Prepare Burger Mixture**: In a bowl, combine mashed black beans, breadcrumbs, grated carrot, corn kernels, BBQ sauce, smoked paprika, salt, and pepper. Mix until well combined.
2. **Form Patties**: Shape the mixture into 4 patties.
3. **Cook Patties**: Heat a skillet over medium heat and cook the patties for 4-5 minutes on each side, until golden brown.
4. **Assemble Burger**: Place the patties on sandwich buns and top with lettuce, tomato, and avocado.
5. **Serve**: Serve immediately.

Vegan Avocado and Tofu Wrap

Ingredients:

- 1 block firm tofu, pressed and sliced
- 1 ripe avocado, sliced
- 1 tbsp soy sauce or tamari
- 1 tbsp olive oil
- 1 tsp garlic powder
- 1/2 tsp smoked paprika
- 1 large whole wheat tortilla
- Fresh spinach or arugula
- 1 tbsp hummus (optional)

Instructions:

1. **Prepare Tofu**: Marinate tofu slices in soy sauce, olive oil, garlic powder, and smoked paprika for 10 minutes.
2. **Cook Tofu**: Heat a skillet over medium heat and cook tofu slices for 3-4 minutes on each side, until golden.
3. **Assemble Wrap**: Lay the tortilla flat and spread hummus (if using). Add tofu slices, avocado, and fresh spinach or arugula.
4. **Wrap and Serve**: Roll up the tortilla to enclose the fillings and serve immediately.

Tempeh Lettuce and Tomato Sandwich

Ingredients:

- 1 block tempeh, sliced
- 1 tbsp soy sauce or tamari
- 1 tbsp olive oil
- 1 tsp smoked paprika
- 4 slices whole grain bread, toasted
- Lettuce and tomato slices
- Vegan mayo or mustard for spread

Instructions:

1. **Cook Tempeh**: Marinate tempeh slices in soy sauce, olive oil, and smoked paprika for 10 minutes. Heat a skillet over medium heat and cook tempeh for 4-5 minutes on each side until golden.
2. **Assemble Sandwich**: Spread vegan mayo or mustard on the toasted bread. Layer with tempeh, lettuce, and tomato slices.
3. **Serve**: Serve immediately.

Veggie "Tuna" Salad Sandwich

Ingredients:

- 1 can chickpeas, drained and mashed
- 2 tbsp vegan mayo
- 1 tbsp Dijon mustard
- 1 tbsp lemon juice
- 1/4 cup diced celery
- 1/4 cup diced red onion
- Salt and pepper to taste
- 4 slices whole grain bread
- Lettuce and tomato slices

Instructions:

1. **Prepare Filling**: Mash chickpeas in a bowl and mix with vegan mayo, Dijon mustard, lemon juice, celery, red onion, salt, and pepper.
2. **Assemble Sandwich**: Spread the veggie "tuna" salad on two slices of bread. Add lettuce and tomato slices.
3. **Serve**: Top with the remaining bread slice and serve immediately.

Portobello and Spinach Burger

Ingredients:

- 4 large Portobello mushroom caps
- 1 tbsp olive oil
- 1 tbsp balsamic vinegar
- Salt and pepper to taste
- 1/2 cup fresh spinach
- 4 sandwich buns
- Vegan mayo or pesto (optional)

Instructions:

1. **Prepare Mushrooms**: Remove the stems from the Portobello mushrooms and drizzle them with olive oil, balsamic vinegar, salt, and pepper.
2. **Cook Mushrooms**: Grill or pan-fry the mushrooms for 4-5 minutes on each side until tender.
3. **Assemble Burger**: Place the cooked mushrooms on sandwich buns. Top with fresh spinach and vegan mayo or pesto.
4. **Serve**: Serve immediately.

Chickpea and Spinach Burger

Ingredients:

- 1 can chickpeas, drained and mashed
- 1/2 cup breadcrumbs
- 1/4 cup cooked spinach, squeezed dry
- 1/4 cup grated carrot
- 1 tbsp nutritional yeast
- 1 tbsp soy sauce or tamari
- 1 tsp garlic powder
- Salt and pepper to taste
- 4 sandwich buns
- Lettuce and tomato for garnish

Instructions:

1. **Prepare Burger Mixture**: In a bowl, combine mashed chickpeas, breadcrumbs, cooked spinach, grated carrot, nutritional yeast, soy sauce, garlic powder, salt, and pepper.
2. **Form Patties**: Shape the mixture into 4 patties.
3. **Cook Patties**: Heat a skillet over medium heat and cook the patties for 4-5 minutes on each side, until golden brown.
4. **Assemble Burger**: Place the patties on sandwich buns and top with lettuce and tomato.
5. **Serve**: Serve immediately.

Vegan Meatball Sub

Ingredients:

- 1 cup cooked lentils
- 1/2 cup breadcrumbs
- 1/4 cup grated carrot
- 1/4 cup chopped fresh parsley
- 2 tbsp tomato paste
- 1 tbsp nutritional yeast
- 1 tsp garlic powder
- Salt and pepper to taste
- 1 cup marinara sauce
- 4 sub rolls
- Vegan mozzarella cheese (optional)

Instructions:

1. **Prepare Meatballs**: In a bowl, combine lentils, breadcrumbs, grated carrot, parsley, tomato paste, nutritional yeast, garlic powder, salt, and pepper. Form into meatballs.
2. **Cook Meatballs**: Heat a skillet over medium heat and cook the meatballs, turning occasionally, for about 10 minutes until golden brown.
3. **Warm Sauce**: In a separate pot, heat the marinara sauce.
4. **Assemble Sub**: Place the meatballs in the sub rolls, pour marinara sauce over them, and sprinkle with vegan mozzarella if using.
5. **Serve**: Serve immediately, with optional extra marinara sauce on the side.

Roasted Carrot and Hummus Sandwich

Ingredients:

- 4 large carrots, peeled and cut into sticks
- 2 tbsp olive oil
- 1 tsp cumin
- Salt and pepper to taste
- 4 slices whole grain bread
- 1/2 cup hummus
- Fresh cilantro or parsley for garnish
- Sliced cucumber and avocado for garnish (optional)

Instructions:

1. **Roast Carrots**: Preheat the oven to 400°F (200°C). Toss carrot sticks in olive oil, cumin, salt, and pepper. Spread them on a baking sheet and roast for 25-30 minutes, turning halfway through, until tender and lightly caramelized.
2. **Assemble Sandwich**: Spread hummus on the toasted bread slices. Layer with roasted carrots, fresh cilantro or parsley, and optional cucumber and avocado slices.
3. **Serve**: Close the sandwich and serve immediately.

Crispy Tofu and Coleslaw Sandwich

Ingredients:

- 1 block firm tofu, pressed and sliced
- 1/2 cup cornstarch
- 1/4 cup soy sauce or tamari
- 1 tbsp rice vinegar
- 1 tsp sesame oil
- 1 tbsp olive oil for frying
- 1 cup shredded cabbage
- 1/4 cup grated carrot
- 1/4 cup vegan mayo
- 1 tbsp apple cider vinegar
- 1 tbsp maple syrup
- 4 sandwich rolls or buns

Instructions:

1. **Prepare Tofu**: Coat tofu slices in cornstarch, then dip in soy sauce, rice vinegar, and sesame oil. Heat olive oil in a pan and fry tofu until golden and crispy on both sides.
2. **Make Coleslaw**: In a bowl, mix shredded cabbage, grated carrot, vegan mayo, apple cider vinegar, and maple syrup. Season with salt and pepper.
3. **Assemble Sandwich**: Layer the crispy tofu slices on the sandwich rolls, then top with coleslaw.
4. **Serve**: Serve immediately for a crunchy and creamy combination.

Black Bean and Quinoa Burger

Ingredients:

- 1 can black beans, drained and mashed
- 1 cup cooked quinoa
- 1/4 cup breadcrumbs
- 1 tbsp nutritional yeast
- 1/4 cup finely chopped onion
- 1 clove garlic, minced
- 1 tbsp soy sauce or tamari
- 1 tsp cumin
- Salt and pepper to taste
- 4 burger buns
- Lettuce, tomato, and avocado for garnish

Instructions:

1. **Prepare Burger Mixture**: In a bowl, combine mashed black beans, cooked quinoa, breadcrumbs, nutritional yeast, chopped onion, garlic, soy sauce, cumin, salt, and pepper. Mix until well combined.
2. **Form Patties**: Shape the mixture into 4 patties.
3. **Cook Patties**: Heat a skillet over medium heat and cook the patties for 4-5 minutes on each side until golden brown.
4. **Assemble Burger**: Place the patties on burger buns and top with lettuce, tomato, and avocado.
5. **Serve**: Serve immediately.

Vegan Buffalo Cauliflower Sandwich

Ingredients:

- 1 medium cauliflower, cut into florets
- 1/2 cup flour
- 1/2 cup plant-based milk
- 1 cup breadcrumbs
- 1/4 cup hot sauce
- 1 tbsp olive oil
- 4 sandwich buns
- Lettuce, tomato, and vegan ranch dressing for garnish

Instructions:

1. **Prepare Cauliflower**: Preheat the oven to 425°F (220°C). In a bowl, whisk together flour and plant-based milk to make a batter. Dip cauliflower florets in the batter, then coat with breadcrumbs.
2. **Bake Cauliflower**: Spread the coated cauliflower florets on a baking sheet and bake for 20-25 minutes, flipping halfway through, until crispy.
3. **Buffalo Sauce**: In a separate bowl, mix hot sauce and olive oil. Once the cauliflower is baked, toss it in the buffalo sauce.
4. **Assemble Sandwich**: Place the buffalo cauliflower on the sandwich buns and top with lettuce, tomato, and vegan ranch dressing.
5. **Serve**: Serve immediately for a spicy, crispy delight.

Grilled Tofu and Veggie Wrap

Ingredients:

- 1 block firm tofu, pressed and sliced
- 1 tbsp olive oil
- 1 tsp smoked paprika
- 1 tsp garlic powder
- 1/2 tsp cumin
- Salt and pepper to taste
- 1/2 cup hummus
- 1 cup mixed greens
- 1/2 cucumber, sliced
- 1/2 avocado, sliced
- 1/4 cup shredded carrots
- 4 whole wheat wraps

Instructions:

1. **Prepare Tofu**: In a bowl, toss tofu slices with olive oil, smoked paprika, garlic powder, cumin, salt, and pepper. Heat a grill pan over medium heat and cook tofu for 3-4 minutes on each side until grill marks appear.
2. **Assemble Wrap**: Spread hummus on the center of each wrap. Layer with grilled tofu, mixed greens, cucumber, avocado, and shredded carrots.
3. **Wrap and Serve**: Roll up the wraps tightly, slice in half, and serve immediately.

Smoky Chickpea Burger

Ingredients:

- 1 can chickpeas, drained and mashed
- 1/2 cup breadcrumbs
- 1/4 cup finely chopped onion
- 1 clove garlic, minced
- 1 tbsp smoked paprika
- 1 tbsp tahini
- 1 tbsp soy sauce or tamari
- 1/2 tsp cumin
- Salt and pepper to taste
- 4 burger buns
- Lettuce, tomato, and vegan mayo for garnish

Instructions:

1. **Prepare Burger Mixture**: In a bowl, combine mashed chickpeas, breadcrumbs, onion, garlic, smoked paprika, tahini, soy sauce, cumin, salt, and pepper. Mix until well combined.
2. **Form Patties**: Shape the mixture into 4 patties.
3. **Cook Patties**: Heat a skillet over medium heat and cook the patties for 3-4 minutes on each side until golden brown and crispy.
4. **Assemble Burger**: Place the patties on burger buns and top with lettuce, tomato, and vegan mayo.
5. **Serve**: Serve immediately for a smoky, satisfying burger.

Cauliflower and Chickpea Sandwich

Ingredients:

- 1/2 cauliflower, cut into florets
- 1 can chickpeas, drained and mashed
- 2 tbsp olive oil
- 1 tsp garlic powder
- 1 tsp paprika
- Salt and pepper to taste
- 4 slices whole grain bread
- 1/2 avocado, sliced
- Fresh parsley for garnish
- Vegan mayo for spread (optional)

Instructions:

1. **Roast Cauliflower**: Preheat the oven to 400°F (200°C). Toss cauliflower florets with olive oil, garlic powder, paprika, salt, and pepper. Roast for 25-30 minutes, flipping halfway, until tender and slightly crispy.
2. **Prepare Chickpeas**: In a bowl, mash the chickpeas with a fork or potato masher until chunky.
3. **Assemble Sandwich**: Spread vegan mayo on the toasted bread slices. Layer with mashed chickpeas, roasted cauliflower, avocado slices, and fresh parsley.
4. **Serve**: Close the sandwich and serve immediately.

Seitan and Avocado Burger

Ingredients:

- 1 cup seitan, sliced
- 1 tbsp olive oil
- 1 tbsp soy sauce or tamari
- 1 tsp smoked paprika
- 1/2 avocado, sliced
- 1/4 cup vegan mayo
- 4 burger buns
- Lettuce, tomato, and pickles for garnish

Instructions:

1. **Cook Seitan**: Heat olive oil in a skillet over medium heat. Add seitan slices, soy sauce, smoked paprika, and cook for 4-5 minutes, flipping occasionally, until lightly crispy.
2. **Assemble Burger**: Spread vegan mayo on the burger buns. Place the cooked seitan slices on the bottom buns, and top with avocado, lettuce, tomato, and pickles.
3. **Serve**: Serve immediately for a flavorful, protein-packed burger.

Vegan Lentil Burger

Ingredients:

- 1 cup cooked lentils
- 1/4 cup breadcrumbs
- 1/4 cup finely chopped onion
- 1/4 cup grated carrot
- 1 tbsp soy sauce or tamari
- 1 tsp garlic powder
- 1 tsp cumin
- Salt and pepper to taste
- 4 burger buns
- Lettuce, tomato, and mustard for garnish

Instructions:

1. **Prepare Burger Mixture**: In a bowl, combine cooked lentils, breadcrumbs, onion, grated carrot, soy sauce, garlic powder, cumin, salt, and pepper. Mix well until it holds together.
2. **Form Patties**: Shape the mixture into 4 patties.
3. **Cook Patties**: Heat a skillet over medium heat with a little oil. Cook the patties for 4-5 minutes on each side until golden brown.
4. **Assemble Burger**: Place the lentil patties on the burger buns and top with lettuce, tomato, and mustard.
5. **Serve**: Serve immediately for a hearty, flavorful burger.

www.ingramcontent.com/pod-product-compliance
Lightning Source LLC
LaVergne TN
LVHW081502060526
838201LV00056BA/2895